# The World of Scales

Don J. Maclean

AGOGIC PUBLISHING
www. agogic.biz

Text editing by: Jeneane McKenzie

**National Library of Canada Cataloguing in Publication**

MacLean, Don J., 1968-
The world of scales : a compendium of scales for all instruments / Don J. MacLean ; Jeneane McKenzie, editor. -- 2nd ed.

Includes index.
ISBN 1-896595-21-9

1. Musical intervals and scales. I. McKenzie, Jeneane, 1968- II. Title.
MT45.M163 2003          781.246          C2002-911263-X

Quantity discounts are available on bulk purchases of this book for educational purposes. For information please contact Agogic Publishing 406-109 Tenth Street, New Westminster, British Columbia, V3M 3X7, (604) 290-2692.

Visit us on our website:
http://www.agogic.biz
for free downloads
and product information.

# Acknowledgements

*This book is dedicated to all of my students both past and present, and to those I have not had the privilege to teach personally. I hope you will gain many new and exciting insights into this sublime and profound art we call music.*

I WOULD LIKE TO thank my students and teaching colleagues for their input as this book evolved into its present form. I must also thank all of my teachers/professors from Humber College and York University for feeding my quest for knowledge—this learning experience provided the impetus to explore many areas of music I did not even know existed.

Special thanks go to Jeneane for all of her encouragement, patience and support.

# About the Author

Don J. MacLean is an active freelance guitarist, composer and educator. His musical training includes studies at the Royal Conservatory of Music, Humber College, and York University, where he obtained his B.A. (Dbl. Hons. Maj.) in music and psychology. His twenty years of teaching, performing and composing have made Don a highly sought-after expert for workshops, seminars and master classes.

Don J. MacLean is the author of:

**The World of Scales: A Compendium of Scales for the Modern Guitar Player**
**The World of Scales: A Compendium of Scales for all Instruments**

**Guitar Essentials: The Chord Master**
**Guitar Essentials: Scale Master 1**
**Guitar Essentials: Improviser**

**Music Essentials: Improviser**

**Fit Fingers Book 1**
**Fit Fingers Book 2**

**Quick Tips for Fast Fingers**
**Quick Tips: Basic Chords for Guitar**
**Quick Tips: Basic Scales for Guitar**

**Mega Chops: Mozart for Electric Guitar**
**Mega Chops: Bach for Electric Guitar**
**Mega Chops: Corelli for Electric Guitar**
**Mega Chops: Vivaldi for Electric Guitar**

# Contents

## Chapter 1          What are Scales?

## Chapter 2          Patterns

## Chapter 3          Chord Construction

## Chapter 4        Tetratonic Scales

## Chapter 5        Pentatonic Scales

## Chapter 6    Hexatonic Scales

# Chapter 7      Heptatonic Scales

# Chapter 8        Miscellany

# Preface

WHEN I BEGAN AS a music instructor, I frequently encountered questions about the modes and non-traditional scales. I would refer my students to three or four books for explanations, but they would always return and ask the questions again.

The World of Scales began as my teaching manual for scale studies. Over the years, it has evolved into the text that you hold in your hands—a comprehensive scale study with emphasis on the construction and application of scales. Modes, often an area of confusion, are covered in detail and the concept of modalization is fully explained

The World of Scales is designed for musicians of all levels. All of the theoretical principles necessary for a thorough understanding of scales are covered in this book.

I hope you enjoy your exploration of the many scales the world has to offer.

Don J. MacLean

# Introduction

SCALES ARE MANIFEST IN most forms of music found throughout the world. Just as there are a plethora of unique cultures, there are equally as many diverse approaches to the making of music. Some closely related cultures share pitch systems, while other cultures use pitch systems with little in common.

With the continuing proliferation of technology, multi-culturalism, and the mass media, contemporary musicians are able to view the world's music (both past and present) with an unprecedented scope of detail. Contemporary musicians are able to listen to recordings or even witness live performances of indigenous musics that were in the not so distance past, completely inaccessible.

With even a cursory examination of the history of Western Art music, one can see numerous occurrences of composers that were directly influenced by the music of other cultures. In many cases these composers would fuse these sometimes divergent musical practices and assimilate them into a "new" musical style. In other instances, pieces were written to evoke the sounds of these "newly found" musical practices.

The early Twentieth Century witnessed an influx of non-European musical practices. A well-known example of this occurred in 1889, when Claude Debussy attended the Paris International Exhibition. He was awe-struck by the hauntingly beautiful pentatonic and whole-tone melodies of an Indonesian gamelan orchestra and, as a result, Debussy began employing a number of different scales in his compositions—significantly enriching his music.

This book is a compendium of the many scales the world has to offer. This is by no means complete in the sense of listing every scale ever used or theorized (if it did it would be an exceptionally thick book), but it does cover the most common and intriguing scales of the world. These scales are essential to all composers, and improvising musicians who have an unquenchable thirst for knowledge.

# How To Use This Book

The best approach is to read the first three chapters of this text to gain a basic theoretical knowledge. Your next step should be to proceed through the rest of this book and discover the scales that interest you the most.

It is highly recommended that you periodically play all of the scales presented in this text. As your musical skills advance, you will also note a marked change in your musical taste. A scale that you may find highly dissonant today, could very well become your favourite scale a month or a year later.

After you have selected the scales that you like, your task is to become proficient playing these scales on your instrument. At first you should practice all scales ascending and descending. Then proceed to practice patterns that make use of these scales. Chapter 2 is devoted to some of the many possible patterns. As many musicians find practicing scales tedious, creativity is the key consideration here. Use the patterns given to help you find and build your own melodic ideas. As you practice these scales in patterns you will begin to truly "hear" each scale—this will ultimately allow you more freedom to utilize each scale to its full potential. To maximize your technical abilities on your instrument, you should incorporate as many of these scales as possible into your daily practice routine.

# Chapter 1 — What are Scales?

A SCALE IS A collection of pitches that have been arranged into a specific ascending and descending order. The ascending form of a scale may vary from that of its descending version. The ascending and descending forms of some scales can occasionally vary quite dramatically, with some cultures making use of scales that exploit completely different notes (or vary the intonation so as to procure a half-sharp or half-flat) in the descending version of the scale.

The smallest standard distance between any two given notes in the West, is the semitone. There are a total of twelve semitones in an octave.[1] This means there are a total of twelve notes in the West that can be arranged to form scales. For the sake of comparison, it is quite common for instruments in India to make use of an octave that has been divided into 22 parts. This accounts for the vast number of scales called *ragas*, that are ubiquitous in Indian music. In contrast, the Indonesians have two main pitch systems, called *Sléndro* and *Pélog*. Indonesian instruments are tuned to one or the other of these systems. Sléndro divides the octave into five parts. Of these five parts, only the root note can be accurately played on an instrument tuned to the equal tempered system used in the West.

In the Western world most of our musical styles are based on a closed system of pitches (i.e., the octave being divided into 12 equal divisions). The twelve notes of the octave are grouped into specific arrangements of pitches to form scales. The most common groupings are scales that contain five or seven notes (other groupings are possible and are examined later in this text).

Some Twentieth Century composers, have made extensive use of intervals smaller than the semitone.[2] Others have worked with some of the many possible permutations of the 12 available notes found in equal tempered tuning and developed a compositional procedure called *Twelve Tone Technique*. (There are 479,001,600 possible arrangements of 12 notes.)

The scales that will concern us are those that can accurately (or at least with relative accuracy) be duplicated on an instrument tuned to equal temperament.

*Equal Temperament* is basically the standard system for tuning instruments in the West. This system of tuning makes all semitones essentially the same size. If you were to use other systems of tuning, such as *Mean Tone* or *Pythagorean*, the result would be varying sizes of semitones.

---

[1] An octave is the distance you must travel to reach a repeat of any one given note. For example, if you were to travel from C to C (C D E F G A B C), you would have traveled the distance of an octave. See the section on intervals for more details.

[2] Any interval smaller than a semitone is usually referred to as a *microtone*.

Scales tend to be used as a basis for compositions or as a vehicle for improvisation. The *major scale* is often used for the derivation of many of the theoretical principles in Western music theory. Consequently, this will be the first scale to be examined.

# The Major Scale

In order to have a *major scale*, there must be a specific arrangement of semitones and whole tones. The C major scale consists of the following notes:

$$C \quad D \quad E \quad F \quad G \quad A \quad B \quad C$$

T = Whole Tone: A whole tone is the distance of two semitones. The whole tone is also referred to by some as a *tone* or a *whole step*.

S = Semitone: The semitone is also known as a *half step*.

$$C \;_T\; D \;_T\; E \;_S\; F \;_T\; G \;_T\; A \;_T\; B \;_S\; C$$

To build any major scale simply proceed through the following progression of semitones and whole tones:

# Major Scale Formula: T T S T T T S

Here is a listing of all of the major scales.

| Table of Major Scales | |
|---|---|
| C major | C D E F G A B C |
| G major | G A B C D E $F^\#$ G |
| D major | D E $F^\#$ G A B $C^\#$ D |
| A major | A B $C^\#$ D E $F^\#$ $G^\#$ A |
| E major | E $F^\#$ $G^\#$ A B $C^\#$ $D^\#$ E |
| B major | B $C^\#$ $D^\#$ E $F^\#$ $G^\#$ $A^\#$ B |
| $F^\#$ major | $F^\#$ $G^\#$ $A^\#$ B $C^\#$ $D^\#$ $E^\#$ $F^\#$ |
| $C^\#$ major | $C^\#$ $D^\#$ $E^\#$ $F^\#$ $G^\#$ $A^\#$ $B^\#$ $C^\#$ |
| F major | F G A $B^b$ C D E F |
| $B^b$ major | $B^b$ C D $E^b$ F G A $B^b$ |
| $E^b$ major | $E^b$ F G $A^b$ $B^b$ C D $E^b$ |
| $A^b$ major | $A^b$ $B^b$ C $D^b$ $E^b$ F G $A^b$ |
| $D^b$ major | $D^b$ $E^b$ F $G^b$ $A^b$ $B^b$ C $D^b$ |
| $G^b$ major | $G^b$ $A^b$ $B^b$ $C^b$ $D^b$ $E^b$ F $G^b$ |
| $C^b$ major | $C^b$ $D^b$ $E^b$ $F^b$ $G^b$ $A^b$ $B^b$ $C^b$ |

Roman numerals are usually used to represent the scale degrees of any scale. The traditional method of numbering a scale, employed upper case Roman numerals for the first, fourth, and fifth notes of that scale. The first, fourth and fifth degrees tend to be the basic pillars of Western Art Music. These notes are considered to be very important in establishing a sense of key and are quite important for the operation of functional harmony. The use of Roman numerals is gradually changing. Jazz theorists still use Roman numerals but some now favour upper case numerals for all of the notes in a scale. The primary reason for this is the increase in the importance of chords built on the second, third and seventh degrees in contemporary Jazz. We will use Roman numerals and Arabic numerals interchangeably.

| C | D | E | F | G | A | B | C |
|---|---|---|---|---|---|---|---|
| I | ii | iii | IV | V | vi | vii | VIII (or I) |

# Intervals

An *interval* is the distance between any two given notes. To determine the size of an interval, simply count from the lower note to the upper note of the interval. When you count up, remember to number the starting note as one. For example, if you were going to determine the distance between the notes F and E (the F is lower pitched than the E in this example), you would arrive at the distance of a seventh.

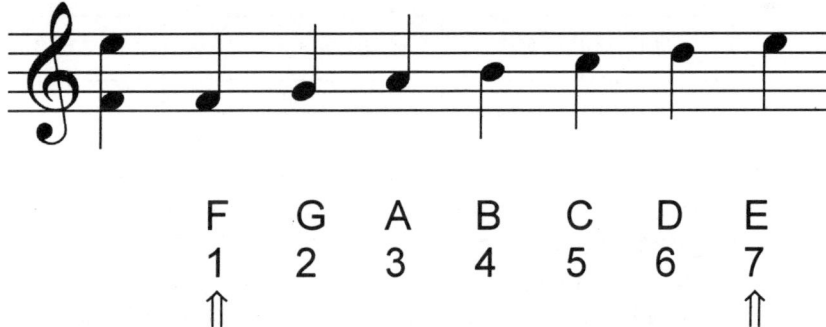

| F | G | A | B | C | D | E |
|---|---|---|---|---|---|---|
| 1 | 2 | 3 | 4 | 5 | 6 | 7 |
| ⇑ | | | | | | ⇑ |

After you have determined the distance between the two notes, you must now determine the interval's quality. You now compare the upper note to see if it is contained in the major scale of the lower note. If the upper note is contained in the major scale of the lower note (i.e., if the E is contained in the F major scale in the above example), you have a *diatonic interval*. As you can see, the E is contained in the F major scale. This means that this would be considered to be a diatonic interval.

The diatonic intervals of a major scale are: the *perfect unison, major second, major third, perfect fourth, perfect fifth, major sixth, major seventh* and the *perfect octave.*

# Interval Classification

The unison,[3] fourth, fifth and the octave (8th) are considered to be *perfect intervals.* If a perfect interval is raised by one semitone, it becomes an *augmented interval.* A perfect interval lowered by one semitone will become a *diminished interval.*

Each move to the left or right represents the distance of one semitone.

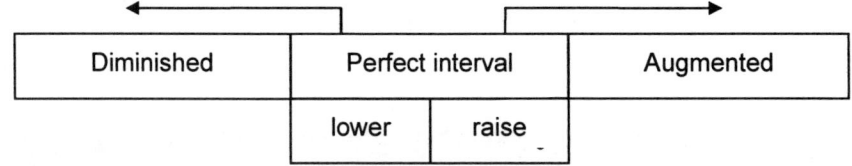

The remaining intervals, the second, third, sixth and the seventh are considered to be *major* intervals, if the upper note of the interval is contained in the major scale of the lower note. If a major interval is lowered by one semitone, it becomes a *minor* interval. A lowered minor interval, becomes a *diminished* interval. If a major interval is raised, it will be called an *augmented* interval.

Each move to the left or right represents the distance of one semitone.

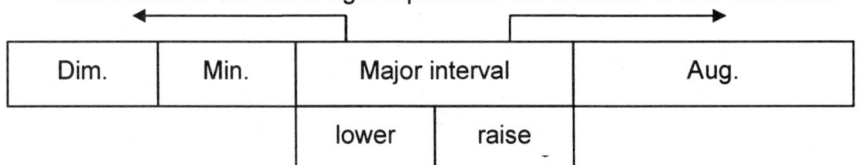

The preceding discussion of intervals dealt with *simple intervals.* A simple interval is an interval that is no larger than an octave. Any interval that is larger than an octave is deemed to be a *compound interval.*

The only compound intervals you will need for this book (specifically for the section that details chord construction) are the ninth, eleventh and thirteenth. To determine these intervals, simply extend the major scale up one additional octave.

---

[3] The unison is the sounding of the same note twice.

In terms of letter names, you will find that the second and ninth, fourth and eleventh, and the sixth and the thirteenth are interchangeable. The only difference between a ninth above C and second above C is that the ninth is an octave above the second.

$$2 \Rightarrow 9$$
$$4 \Rightarrow 11$$
$$6 \Rightarrow 13$$

Compound intervals take on the same quality as their simple interval counterparts. A major second above C is the note D. A major 9th above C is also a D. Just as you can have an aug 2nd, min 2nd or a dim 2nd; you can therefore have an aug 9th, min 9th or a dim 9th.

A *scale degree* is a number used to identify any note's position in a scale. For example, the fourth scale degree is the fourth note found in a scale. A lowered scale degree will be indicated by a flat [(b)] symbol and a raised scale degree will be indicated with a sharp [(#)] symbol. Any natural notes will be indicated with the abbreviation [(nat)] or the number will have no indication beside it. Here are two different ways to write the same scale.

Spanish Dominant:

| 1 | $^b$2 | $^b$3 | 3$^{(nat.)}$ | 5 | $^b$6 | $^b$7 |
|---|---|---|---|---|---|---|

or:

| 1 | $^b$2 | $^b$3 | 3 | 5 | $^b$6 | $^b$7 |
|---|---|---|---|---|---|---|

One important point must be emphasized with regard to the preceding study of intervals: THIS IS AN EXTREME SIMPLIFICATION OF INTERVALS. We are merely concerned with the theoretical principals necessary for using this text. If you are not comfortable with intervals after the preceding explanation, you should consult any of the numerous theory textbooks available.

Notation of some scales can become a very difficult area due to enharmonic equivalent[4] intervals. Most heptatonic scales are preferably notated

---

[4]Enharmonic equivalents are notes that are written differently but sound the same. In equal tempered tuning G$^b$ and F$^\#$ sound the same even although the two notes have different letter-names.

with seven different letter-names. If we were to follow this, the Spanish Dominant scale would be spelled as follows:

Spanish Dominant:
$$1 \quad {}^{b}2 \quad {}^{b}3 \quad {}^{b}4 \quad 5 \quad {}^{b}6 \quad {}^{b}7$$

The $^{b}4$ (diminished fourth) is not a very common interval so when it is used, it can create some confusion. To simplify things, we will tend to favor the natural 3 instead of the $^{b}4$ notation in this case. The $^{b}3$ can be thought of as a $^{\#}9$ which would be written as a $^{\#}2$. You now would have:

Spanish Dominant:
$$1 \quad {}^{b}2 \quad {}^{\#}2 \quad 3 \quad 5 \quad {}^{b}6 \quad {}^{b}7$$

The above notation considers some of the harmonic possibilities of the scale (for a more extensive examination of this topic see Chapter 3).

As you can see there are many ways to notate any of the scales presented in this book. Do not become unnecessarily concerned with all of these possible notations. Your primary objective should be to understand one notational possibility and know it well. The others should be easily extractable.

To examine each scale, and make it easier to remember, we will compare each of the scales in this text to the major scale. This is also a great way for you to quickly hear the differences between each scale.

Let us now look at a comparison of one of the scales you will find in this text to the major scale. The *Harmonic Major* scale consists of the following notes: C D E F G A$^{b}$ B C. When this scale is compared to the major scale **(we will always compare the new scale to a major scale built on the same starting pitch)**: C D E F G A B C, we see the A is the only altered note. Our formula for the Harmonic Major scale will therefore be: 1 2 3 4 5 $^{b}$6 7. If you want to build a Harmonic Major scale on a B$^{b}$, you would start with the B$^{b}$ major scale and alter the necessary notes.

B$^{b}$ major:

$$B^{b} \quad C \quad D \quad E^{b} \quad F \quad G \quad A \quad B^{b}$$

The formula for the Harmonic Major scale calls for a $^b$6 so, you simply lower the sixth degree one semitone and you will have a B$^b$ Harmonic Major scale.

B$^b$ Harmonic Major:

# Identification of Scales

There is currently no standard or uniform system employed throughout the world to identify scales by name. There are numerous names used for some scales. For example, the *Lydian* $^b$7 scale is also referred to as *Lydian Dominant*, *Mixolydian* $^#$4, or the *Overtone scale*. This obviously creates some difficulties when one is discussing scales. Given the multiplicity of possible names of any one given scale, it is best to learn the scales presented here without being overly dependent on names.

Scale names are often determined by:
I. The geographical region in which the scale is typically employed,
II. The geographical area one lives in, or;
III. The institution(s) and or teachers with whom one has studied.

This can quite obviously create confusion among different musicians, so it is quite prudent for us to de-emphasize the names of these scales in favor of the mechanics behind them. With this in mind, we will still look at some of the more common names for each scale discussed in this text but, most importantly, we will examine the construction of each scale. If you are aware of the intervallic configuration of each scale, you are more apt to understand some of the possible synonyms for these scales. Most importantly however, if you are fully aware of their structure you are more likely to see some of the many applications for these scales. For example, if you were aware of the construction of the following scale: 1 $^b$2 3 4 5 $^b$6 $^b$7, you would be more likely to realize some of its many uses. This scale can be used over a Dominant 7 chord that contains a $^b$9 and or a $^b$13 as its upper extensions. If you were only aware that this scale is sometimes referred to as the *Hejaz* scale, you would most likely not be fully aware of its possible applications. This scale is also synonymously known as *Mixolydian* $^b$9 $^b$13, *Phrygian Major*, *Phrygian Dominant*, *Spanish*, and as the *Gypsy scale*. As you can see in some instances scale names can be quite beneficial. The Mixolydian $^b$9 $^b$13 scale by its very name clearly indicates one of its possible uses. This scale can be used in a situation where you would normally utilize a *Mixolydian* scale, but the regular Dominant 7 chord contains a $^b9$ and $^b13$. It is, however, beyond the scope of this book to deal with improvisation or composition in any real depth. The chief purpose of this text is to act as a reference book for scales. The section on chord-scale relationships will give you a good overview of how scales work with chords. For a handy reference of chord-scale relationships see *Music Essentials: Improviser* (ISBN 1-896595-23-5).

The scales that follow can be grouped into many categories:
    I.  By geographical origin,
    II.  By culture-specific names or;
    III. Simply the number of notes in the scale.

In order to lessen the confusion of scale origins (especially since many parts of the world share the same scales), the scales in this text have been categorized for the most part by the number of notes in each scale. (Some of the pentatonic scales have been named by their geographical origin simply because there are no other widely known names for them.)

When you look at some scale names, you may become unnecessarily confused. Just remember that $2 \Leftrightarrow 9, 4 \Leftrightarrow 11, 6 \Leftrightarrow 13$, are interchangeable in scale names. The Mixolydian $^b13$ scale can also be called Mixolydian $^b6$. You should also note that there are numerous scales that have been given the same names but are really very different scales. Take the Hungarian Gypsy scale as a case in point. Some will say that the scale is constructed as: 1 2 $^b3$ $^{\#}4$ 5 $^b6$ 7 and others will say that the scale is : 1 2 $^b3$ $^{\#}4$ 5 $^b6$ $^b7$. So, as you go through this book, you will find some repetitions of scale names for some widely varying scales—this is not a mistake but rather is a perfect example of some of the problems encountered with the current method of naming scales. To make this easier to understand, these scales have been numbered (Hungarian Gypsy No. 1, Hungarian Gypsy No. 2 ,etc.). In other cases, additional names for each scale have been included in parentheses.

# Modalization

Modalization is a technique whereby each note of a scale can become the root note of another scale. The result is simply a re-arrangement of the original scale's intervals. For the Dorian mode, you simply take the major scale and re-write it beginning on the second note. For example if you re-write the C major scale so it commences on the second degree (D), you would have a D Dorian scale.

| C major: | C | D | E | F | G | A | B | C |
|---|---|---|---|---|---|---|---|---|
| D Dorian: | D | E | F | G | A | B | C | D |

Although the D Dorian and the C major scale contain the same notes, there are many differences between them. The C major scale consists of the following arrangement of whole and half steps: T T S T T T S. The Dorian mode consists of: T S T T T S T. In tonal music the two most important notes are the *tonic* (I) and *dominant* (V). The tonic and dominant in C major are the notes C and G respectively. The tonic and dominant notes in D Dorian are D and A. A composition in D Dorian will usually make extensive use of the notes D and A. A melody in C major will emphasize the notes C and G. The tonic and dominant are the most important notes in a scale, while others are related but vary in importance. You will also find that the melodic tendencies of notes will often change as will their individual importance. Melodic tendencies are the natural resolutions of notes. All notes in a scale will appear to be active or stable. The degree of tension or stability is determined by intervallic relationships within the scale. For example, the B in the C major scale will often move to the C, while the F will usually tend to gravitate towards the E.

Certain culturally derived psychological associations will also arise when you modalize any scale. The major scale tends to have a rather happy sound while the Dorian mode tends to be somewhat melancholy. Generally, the scales that have numerous lowered degrees, will tend to have a darker sound than those with comparatively more raised degrees.

For example, the *Locrian* scale has a much darker sound than the *Lydian Augmented* scale:

**Locrian:**

| 1 | $^b2$ | $^b3$ | 4 | $^b5$ | $^b6$ | $^b7$ |
|---|---|---|---|---|---|---|
| C | $D^b$ | $E^b$ | F | $G^b$ | $A^b$ | $B^b$ |

**Lydian Augmented:**

| 1 | 2 | 3 | $^\#4$ | $^\#5$ | 6 | 7 |
|---|---|---|---|---|---|---|
| C | D | E | $F^\#$ | $G^\#$ | A | B |

This quite obviously can become an important detail for composers to consider. If a composer is looking to write music that is ethereal, the scale(s) used would be quite different from those used for a composition that was intended to be menacing. If you are playing over predetermined chord progressions you are usually limited to the appropriate chord-scale relationships.

When you divide a scale into its modes, the most important point to remember is that when you re-write the scale beginning on each of its notes, you must include any of the accidentals present in the scale.

# Diatonic Modes

The modes from a scale will sometimes have standardized names such as those from the major scale.

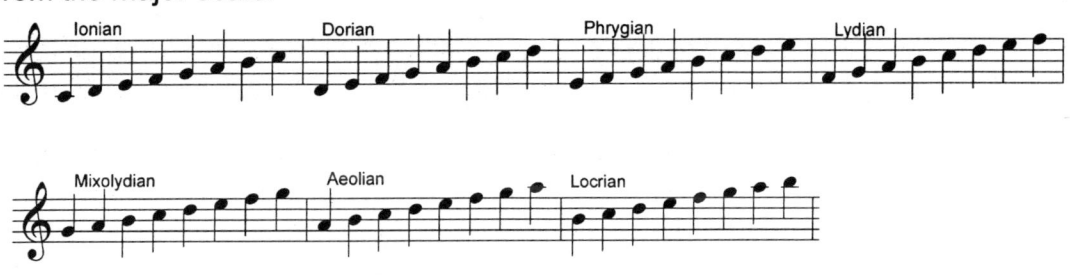

| | | | | | | | | |
|---|---|---|---|---|---|---|---|---|
| C | D | E | F | G | A | B | C | Ionian |
| D | E | F | G | A | B | C | D | Dorian |
| E | F | G | A | B | C | D | E | Phrygian |
| F | G | A | B | C | D | E | F | Lydian |
| G | A | B | C | D | E | F | G | Mixolydian |
| A | B | C | D | E | F | G | A | Aeolian |
| B | C | D | E | F | G | A | B | Locrian |

| | |
|---|---|
| **Mode I** | **Ionian** |
| **Mode ii** | **Dorian** |
| **Mode iii** | **Phrygian** |
| **Mode IV** | **Lydian** |
| **Mode V** | **Mixolydian** |
| **Mode vi** | **Aeolian** |
| **Mode vii** | **Locrian** |

*I Dont Play Like My Aunt Lorraine*

The Diatonic Modes are commonly referred to as the Ecclesiastical Modes, Greek Modes, or the Church Modes. The names of the individual modes are the names of Greek provinces or ancient tribes of people. These scales are by far the most commonly utilized modes found in improvisation. You will hear these scales used in a wide variety of musics such as folk, country, rock and jazz to name but a few. The musica ficta modes that follow are not as common, but are quite prevalent in jazz.

# The Musica Ficta Modes

As discussed earlier, modes can be extracted from any scale. The modes from the *harmonic* and *melodic minor* scales are quite common in jazz improvisation and are sometimes referred to as the *Musica Ficta Modes*. These scales have no standardized names. Due to their level of usage and practical applications, the musica ficta modes warrant a somewhat detailed examination. Before we begin our examination of the Musica Ficta Modes, we must examine the concept of *relative minor scales*. The Aeolian mode is also called the relative minor scale (this scale is also called the ancient minor, pure minor, natural minor, or sometimes just the minor scale). To form a relative minor scale, go to the vi degree of the major scale and re-write the scale (including any accidentals) commencing on this sixth note.

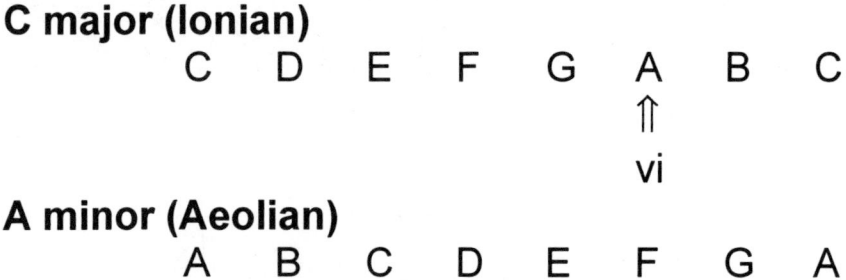

### C major (Ionian)

C   D   E   F   G   A   B   C

⇑

vi

### A minor (Aeolian)

A   B   C   D   E   F   G   A

Here is a table of all of the natural minor scales.

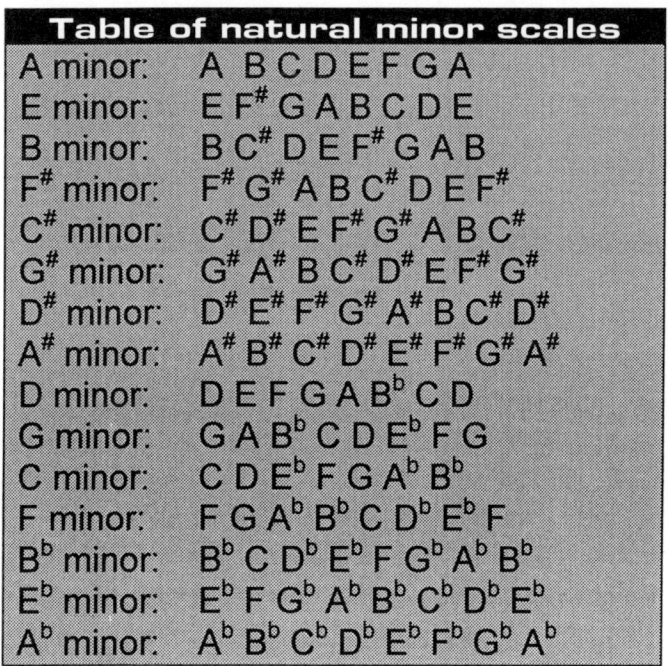

| Table of natural minor scales | |
|---|---|
| A minor: | A B C D E F G A |
| E minor: | E F# G A B C D E |
| B minor: | B C# D E F# G A B |
| F# minor: | F# G# A B C# D E F# |
| C# minor: | C# D# E F# G# A B C# |
| G# minor: | G# A# B C# D# E F# G# |
| D# minor: | D# E# F# G# A# B C# D# |
| A# minor: | A# B# C# D# E# F# G# A# |
| D minor: | D E F G A B♭ C D |
| G minor: | G A B♭ C D E♭ F G |
| C minor: | C D E♭ F G A♭ B♭ |
| F minor: | F G A♭ B♭ C D♭ E♭ F |
| B♭ minor: | B♭ C D♭ E♭ F G♭ A♭ B♭ |
| E♭ minor: | E♭ F G♭ A♭ B♭ C♭ D♭ E♭ |
| A♭ minor: | A♭ B♭ C♭ D♭ E♭ F♭ G♭ A♭ |

To build a *harmonic minor scale*, raise the vii degree of the minor scale. The term *musica ficta*, literally meaning artificial music, was used to denote a chromatic alteration of a scale degree, hence the designation of these scales as musica ficta scales.

### A minor:

A   B   C   D   E   F   G   A

⇑
vii

### A harmonic minor:

A   B   C   D   E   F   G#   A

⇑
vii

To build a *melodic minor scale*, raise the vi and vii degrees of the minor scale ascending and lower them descending.

### A melodic minor ascending (raise vi & vii):

A   B   C   D   E   F#   G#   A

⇑   ⇑
vi   vii

### A melodic minor descending (lower vi & vii):

A   G   F   E   D   C   B   A

⇑   ⇑
vii   vi

As you can see, the melodic minor scale has a different ascending and descending form.  The descending form is the same as the natural minor scale.  For the purpose of improvisation, the ascending version will yield the most interesting possibilities.  This ascending form is very common in jazz improvisation.  When the melodic minor scale's ascending form (raised vi and vii) is used ascending and descending, you have what is referred to as the *Jazz Minor* or the *Real Melodic Minor scale*.

### A  Jazz Minor:

A    B    C    D    E    F#    G#    A

You may also find it helpful to think of the Jazz Minor scale as being a major scale with a $^b$3.

The major and minor scales (harmonic, melodic and natural minor) have been the most frequently employed scales in Western Art music since around 1685.

Now that you are familiar with harmonic and melodic/jazz minor scales, we will now proceed to extract their respective modes.

# Harmonic Minor Modes

For the following example we will use the A harmonic minor scale.

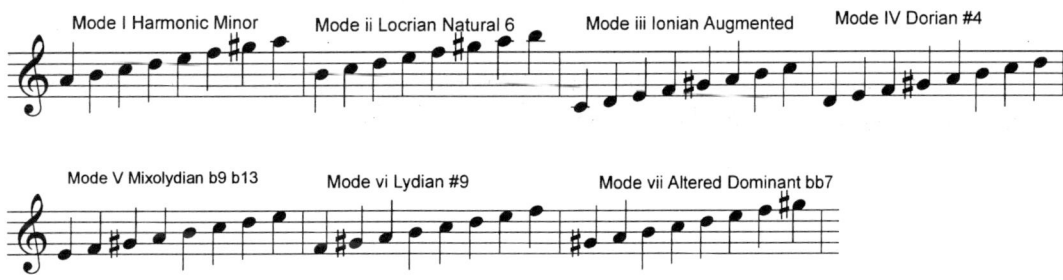

## Mode I    Harmonic Minor:

A  B  C  D  E  F  G$^{\#}$ A

## Mode ii    Locrian Natural 6:

B  C  D  E  F  G$^{\#}$ A  B

## Mode iii    Ionian Augmented:

C  D  E  F  G$^{\#}$ A  B  C

## Mode IV    Dorian $^{\#}$4:

D  E  F  G$^{\#}$ A  B  C  D

## Mode V    Mixolydian $^{b}$9 $^{b}$13:

E  F  G$^{\#}$ A  B  C  D  E

## Mode vi    Lydian $^{\#}$9:

F  G$^{\#}$ A  B  C  D  E  F

## Mode vii    Altered Dominant $^{bb}$7:

G$^{\#}$ A  B  C  D  E  F  G$^{\#}$

The above names are not standardized.  You may prefer to simply refer to each mode by its number, i.e., mode iii, mode V, etc.

# Jazz Minor Modes

The A jazz minor scale will be used for the following example.

**Mode I**     **Jazz Minor:**

A   B   C   D   E   F$^{\#}$ G$^{\#}$ A

**Mode ii**     **Dorian $^{b}$2:**

B   C   D   E   F$^{\#}$ G$^{\#}$ A   B

**Mode iii**     **Lydian Augmented:**

C   D   E   F$^{\#}$ G$^{\#}$ A   B   C

**Mode IV**     **Lydian $^{b}$7:**

D   E   F$^{\#}$ G$^{\#}$ A   B   C   D

## Mode V    Mixolydian $^{b}$13:
E  F$^{\#}$  G$^{\#}$  A  B  C  D  E

## Mode vi    Locrian Natural 9:
F$^{\#}$  G$^{\#}$  A  B  C  D  E  F$^{\#}$

## Mode vii   Altered Dominant:
G$^{\#}$  A  B  C  D  E  F$^{\#}$  G$^{\#}$

Based on the previous discussion, you should now be able to modalize any scale. As you progress through the scales in this book, you will no doubt find many scales you will like. To obtain as much as possible from each scale, you should modalize each of them. You will find that the most common scales that are modes of each other, have been included in this text. For example the most common modes from the Harmonic Major scale are Modes I, iii, IV, and V, all of which can be found in the heptatonic scale section.

# Chapter 2 Patterns

## Intervallic Patterns

SCALES SHOULD BE PRACTICED as many ways as possible. This will not only allow you to stave off the monotony of simply practicing scales ascending and descending, but will also allow you to improve your technique. Practicing a scale only in its ascending and descending forms will provide you with a very limited range of the melodic possibilities that the scale will yield. The most interesting melodic ideas will usually present themselves only with careful experimentation —the exception would be those great ideas that sometimes just appear.

There are many ways to manipulate any scale. The concepts presented in this chapter are a few of the most popular. Entire books have been devoted to these very concepts. The patterns given here, should help you develop thousands of patterns of your own—some of which you may have already heard and others that are quite fresh.

Here are some of the most common patterns you should practice with each scale. The following example uses a C major scale.

**Thirds:**
CE    DF    EG    FA    GB    AC    BD    CE    etc.

**Fourths:**
CF    DG    EA    FB    GC    AD    BE    CF    etc.

Thirds                    Fourths

etc.                    etc.

**Fifths:**

C G   D A   E B   F C   G D   A E   B F   C G   etc.

**Sixths:**

C A   D B   E C   F D   G E   A F   B G   C A   Etc.

Fifths                    Sixths

The preceding patterns are based on certain intervallic configurations. These patterns are diatonic (i.e., there are no notes foreign to the C major scale used in the patterns) and will thus incorporate various sizes of thirds, fourths, fifths or sixths in order to remain within the key. The first pattern shown on the previous page uses thirds. These thirds vary in size from the major third to the minor third in order to stay within the confines of the key: C E (maj 3), D F (min 3), E G (min 3), etc. If you wanted to do this pattern in the key of E major you would have the following notes:

$$E\ G^\#,\ F^\#\ A,\ G^\#\ B,\ A\ C^\#,\ B\ D^\#,\ \text{etc.}$$

# Digital Patterns

A second approach to patterns is to make use of what are sometimes referred to as *digital patterns*. This is when you treat each note as a number, regardless of its true intervallic distance. You would then extract the notes from the scale in the order prescribed by the pattern. For example, the distance from A to C is a minor third. In the A minor pentatonic scale the C is the second note, so if you are deriving digital patterns, the C would be number two in the scale.

A minor pentatonic:

| | A | C | D | E | G | A |
|---|---|---|---|---|---|---|
| Number: | 1 | 2 | 3 | 4 | 5 | 6 (or 1) |
| True intervallic distances: | 1 | min 3 | P4 | P5 | min7 | P8 |

Here are a few of the seemingly infinite number of possible digital patterns:

1 2 3 1, 2 3 4 2, 3 4 5 3, etc.,
1 3 2 1, 2 4 3 2, 3 5 4 3, etc.,
1 2 3 5, 2 3 4 6, 3 4 5 7, etc.,
1 2 5, 2 3 6, 3 4 7, etc.,
1 3 1, 2 4 2, 3 5 3, etc.,
1 3 5, 2 4 6, 3 5 7. etc.,
1 3 5 7, 2 4 6 8, 3 5 7 9, etc.,

You should also note that as you work out some of these possibilities on your own, you will find that some of the patterns utilize arpeggiation (i.e., playing or outlying the notes found in a chord).

# Patterns Derived From Interpolation

Another way to devise some interesting patterns, is to pick the starting note of the scale (1), and a second note two or more consecutive scale degrees higher (numbered from 4 and up). You then fill in the gap that has been artificially created with one of the missing scale degrees.

For example: C-F

| C | D | E | F |
|---|---|---|---|
| 1 | ② | ③ | 4 |

The D or the E can be inserted (interpolated) to form the basis of the next pattern. You then continue this pattern up the rest of the scale.

## Digital pattern 1 ② 4 (interpolating the lower note):

C D F, D E G, E F A, F G B, G A C, A B D, B C E, C D F.

Filling in the gap with the other note will yield the following:

## Digital pattern 1 ③ 4 (interpolating the higher note):

C E F, D F G, E G A, F A B, G B C, A C D, B D E.

Once you have these patterns, you can further manipulate them by inverting the bottom note of each figure:

C D F, D E G, would become: D F C, E G D

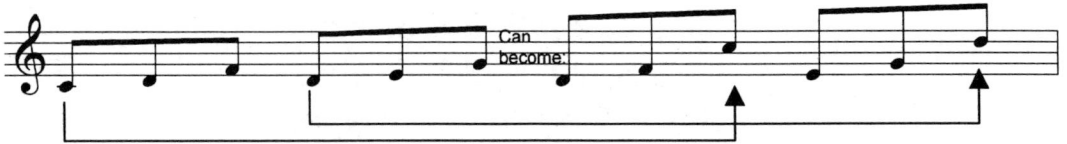

In other words, you move the first note of each grouping of notes up one octave. Once this is done you can repeat the procedure to procure yet another variation:

F C D, G D E—the second inversion

The patterns that follow and those preceding this example should be practiced with each scale.

The first three patterns are based on interpolating one note between a third. Technically there is only one option if you wish to remain within the given key. You should however find the first and second inversions of these patterns to be quite interesting.

## Thirds

C D E, D E F, E F G, F G A, etc.

etc.

**1st inv:**   D E C, E F D, F G E, G A F, etc.

**2nd inv:**   E C D, F D E, G E F, A F G, etc.

# Fourths

C D F, D E G, E F A, F G B, etc.

**1st inv:** D F C, E G D, F A E, G B F, etc.

etc.

**2nd inv:** F C D, G D E, A E F, B F G, etc.

etc.

**Fourths:** C E F, D F G, E G A, F A B, etc.

etc.

**1st inv:** E F C, F G D, G A E, A B F, etc.

etc.

**2nd inv:**  F C E, G D F, A E G, B F A, etc.

# Fifths

C D G, D E A, E F B, F G C, etc.

**1st inv:**  D G C, E A D, F B E, G C F, etc.

**2nd inv:**  G C D, A D E, B E F, C F G, etc.

etc.

**Fifths:**  C E G, D F A, E G B, F A C, etc.

**1st inv:**  E G C, F A D, G B E, A C F, etc.

**2nd inv:**  G C E, A D F, B E G, C F A, etc.

**Fifths:**   C F G, D G A, E A B, F B C, etc.

**1st inv:**   F G C, G A D, A B E, B C F, etc.

**2nd inv:**   G C F, A D G, B E A, C F B, etc.

# Chapter 3 — Chord Construction

EVERY MUSICIAN WILL FIND it very useful to have a good knowledge of chords. If you play a chordal instrument you can obviously play all of the chords found in this section. Those that play monophonic instruments (instruments that can only produce one note at a time) should practice all of the chords dealt with in this section as arpeggios.

Chords can be constructed by stacking consecutive thirds *(tertian)*, fourths *(quartal)*, fifths *(quintal)*, or seconds *(secondal)*.

| Seconds | Thirds | Fourths | Fifths |

Chords are most frequently built by stacking thirds. These tertian-based chords can easily be extracted from any major scale. For a C major chord, you would go to the C major scale and take out the 1st, 3rd, and 5th notes. These notes constitute a major chord. Chords that contain three different notes are called *triads*. To derive any chord, simply go to the major scale of the root note of the chord in question. It does not matter whether you want a D$^b$ major triad or a D$^b$ diminished 7 chord, you would still go to the D$^b$ major scale and extract the appropriate notes.

Here is how to build any chord:
1) Look at the appropriate formula for the chord you want. (See pages 29-31.)
2) Go to the major scale of the chord you want.
3) Extract the necessary notes from the formula.
4) Alter any necessary notes to fit the formula.

The flat $^{(b)}$ symbol means to lower a note by a semitone while the sharp $^{(\#)}$ symbol indicates that the note must be raised by one semitone. As you extract the notes from the major scale be sure to remember the notes that are sharp or flat. If a note is already sharp in the major scale and must be lowered to follow a chord formula, it will become a natural note. The figure on the following page denotes the possible alterations.

| Double Flat[(bb)] | Flat[(b)] | Natural | | Sharp[(#)] | Double Sharp[(x)] |
|---|---|---|---|---|---|
| | | lower | raise | | |
| $D^{bb}$ | $D^{b}$ | D | | $D^{\#}$ | $D^{x}$ |

(Each move to the left or right represents the distance of a semitone.)

Example 1. D minor: Formula $\Rightarrow$ 1 $^{b}$3 5
Take the first, third and fifth notes out of the D major scale.

D major:

| D | E | F$^{\#}$ | G | A | B | C$^{\#}$ | D |
|---|---|---|---|---|---|---|---|
| 1 | 2 | 3 | 4 | 5 | 6 | 7 | 8 |
| ⇑ | | ⇑ | | ⇑ | | | |

For a minor chord, you must lower the third. The F$^{\#}$ will become an F(natural). Therefore the notes in a D minor chord are:

| D | F | A |
|---|---|---|
| 1 | $^{b}$3 | 5 |

Example 2. F$^{\#}$ 7 $^{\#}$5 $^{b}$9:  Formula $\Rightarrow$ 1 3 $^{\#}$5 $^{b}$7 $^{b}$9
Take the first, third, fifth, seventh, and ninth notes out of the F$^{\#}$ major scale.
F$^{\#}$ major:

| F$^{\#}$ | G$^{\#}$ | A$^{\#}$ | B | C$^{\#}$ | D$^{\#}$ | E$^{\#}$ | F$^{\#}$ | G$^{\#}$ |
|---|---|---|---|---|---|---|---|---|
| 1 | 2 | 3 | 4 | 5 | 6 | 7 | 8 | 9 |
| ⇑ | | ⇑ | | ⇑ | | ⇑ | | ⇑ |

For a Dom 7 $^{\#}$5 $^{b}$9 chord, you must raise the fifth, lower the seventh and lower the ninth. The C$^{\#}$ will become a C double sharp (C$^{x}$), the E$^{\#}$ will become a E natural and the G$^{\#}$ will change to a G natural. Therefore the notes in a F$^{\#}$ 7 $^{\#}$5 $^{b}$9 chord are:

| F$^{\#}$ | A$^{\#}$ | C$^{x}$ | E | G |
|---|---|---|---|---|
| 1 | 3 | $^{\#}$5 | $^{b}$7 | $^{b}$9 |

This procedure can be repeated for any of the chords listed in the following formulas. These formulas indicate some of the most common chords that you will encounter.

Just as there is no standardization of scale names from one region to another, there are many problems with the current system of identifying chords. The following abbreviations are used here for simplicity:

> maj $\Rightarrow$ for major
> min $\Rightarrow$ for minor
> dim $\Rightarrow$ for diminished
> sus 4 $\Rightarrow$ for suspended 4
> dom $\Rightarrow$ for dominant

# Triads

| Major | 1 3 5 |
| Minor | 1 $^b$3 5 |
| Diminished | 1 $^b$3 $^b$5 |
| Augmented | 1 3 $^\#$5 |
| Suspended 4 | 1 4 5 |
| Suspended 2 | 1 2 5 |
| Flat 5 | 1 3 $^b$5 |

# Tetrads (Four Part Chords)

| Major 7 | 1 3 5 7 |
| Major 7 $^\#$5 | 1 3 $^\#$5 7 |
| Major 7 $^b$5 | 1 3 $^b$5 7 |
| Dominant 7 | 1 3 5 $^b$7 |
| Dominant 7 $^\#$5 | 1 3 $^\#$5 $^b$7 |
| Dominant 7 $^b$5 | 1 3 $^b$5 $^b$7 |
| Minor Major 7 | 1 $^b$3 5 7 |
| Diminished Major 7 (Minor Major 7 $^b$5) | 1 $^b$3 $^b$5 7 |
| Minor 7 $^b$5 (Half Diminished) | 1 $^b$3 $^b$5 $^b$7 |
| Diminished 7 | 1 $^b$3 $^b$5 $^{bb}$7 |
| Minor 7 | 1 $^b$3 5 $^b$7 |
| Minor 7 $^\#$5 (Minor 7 $^b$6) | 1 $^b$3 $^\#$5/$^b$6 $^b$7 |

| | |
|---|---|
| Dominant 7 sus 4 | 1 4 5 $^b$7 |
| Major 7 sus 4 | 1 4 5 7 |
| Major 6 | 1 3 5 6 |
| Minor 6 | 1 $^b$3 5 6 |
| Major add 9 | 1 3 5 9 |
| Minor add 9 | 1 $^b$3 5 9 |

## Ninth Chords

| | |
|---|---|
| Major 9 | 1 3 5 7 9 |
| Maj 9 $^{\#}$5 | 1 3 $^{\#}$5 7 9 |
| Maj 9 $^b$5 | 1 3 $^b$5 7 9 |
| Dominant 9 | 1 3 5 $^b$7 9 |
| Dom 9 $^b$5 | 1 3 $^b$5 $^b$7 9 |
| Dom 9 $^{\#}$5 | 1 3 $^{\#}$5 $^b$7 9 |
| Dom 7 $^{\#}$9 | 1 3 5 $^b$7 $^{\#}$9 |
| Dom 7 $^b$9 | 1 3 5 $^b$7 $^b$9 |
| Dom 7 $^{\#}$5 $^{\#}$9 | 1 3 $^{\#}$5 $^b$7 $^{\#}$9 |
| Dom 7 $^{\#}$5 $^b$9 | 1 3 $^{\#}$5 $^b$7 $^b$9 |
| Dom 7 $^b$5 $^{\#}$9 | 1 3 $^b$5 $^b$7 $^{\#}$9 |
| Dom 7 $^b$5 $^b$9 | 1 3 $^b$5 $^b$7 $^b$9 |
| Dom 9 sus 4 | 1 4 5 $^b$7 9 |
| Min 9 | 1 $^b$3 5 $^b$7 9 |
| Min 9 maj 7 | 1 $^b$3 5 7 9 |
| Dim maj 9 | 1 $^b$3 $^b$5 7 9 |
| Min 9 $^b$5 | 1 $^b$3 $^b$5 $^b$7 9 |
| Min 6/9 | 1 $^b$3 5 6 9 |
| Maj 6/9 | 1 3 5 6 9 |

## Eleventh Chords

| | |
|---|---|
| Maj 9 $^{\#}$11 | 1 3 5 7 9 $^{\#}$11 |
| Maj 9 $^{\#}$5 $^{\#}$11 | 1 3 $^{\#}$5 7 9 $^{\#}$11 |
| Dom 9 $^{\#}$11 | 1 3 5 $^b$7 9 $^{\#}$11 |
| Dom 7 $^{\#}$9 $^{\#}$11 | 1 3 5 $^b$7 $^{\#}$9 $^{\#}$11 |
| Dom 7 $^b$9 $^{\#}$11 | 1 3 5 $^b$7 $^b$9 $^{\#}$11 |

| | |
|---|---|
| Dom 11 (Dom 9 sus 4) | 1 (3*) 5 $^{b}$7 9 11 |
| Min11 | 1 $^{b}$3 5 $^{b}$7 9 11 |
| Min11 $^{b}$5 | 1 $^{b}$3 $^{b}$5 $^{b}$7 9 11 |

* The major 3rd is usually omitted in a dominant 11 chord due to the strong dissonance created between the third and the eleventh scale degrees. These two notes form a minor 9th interval that usually requires special attention. Because of this, it is usually best to symbolize this chord as a Dom 9 sus 4 so that the third is not present. An augmented 11($^{#}$11) is compatible with a major third, making it the usual choice when an eleventh is added to a Dom 7 chord. This is also why you will not normally encounter a Maj 13 chord with an unaltered 11th. The Major 13 chord usually takes a $^{#}$11 (Maj 13 $^{#}$11).

# Thirteenth Chords

| | |
|---|---|
| Maj 13 $^{#}$11 | 1 3 5 7 9 $^{#}$11 13 |
| Dom 13 $^{#}$11 | 1 3 5 $^{b}$7 9 $^{#}$11 13 |
| Dom 13 sus 4 | 1 4 5 $^{b}$7 9 13 |
| Dom 13 $^{b}$9 | 1 3 5 $^{b}$7 $^{b}$9 13 |
| Dom 13 | 1 3 5 $^{b}$7 9 13 |
| Dom 13 $^{b}$9 sus 4 | 1 4 5 $^{b}$7 $^{b}$9 13 |
| Min13 | 1 $^{b}$3 5 $^{b}$7 9 11 13 |

The preceding formulas give you a basic overview of chord construction. You now have the knowledge to build any of the common chords listed above. The following section will explain how to determine the chords built on any scale and how to use the scales in this book.

# Chord-Scale Relationships

For any chord there will be at least one optimum scale choice. Most chords will have many scale options. Chord-scale relationships can get quite complex and do require a good theoretical knowledge. We will take a very brief and simplified approach to this issue.

To determine the optimum scale choice, the most accurate procedure is to determine the function of the chord. If the chord in question is a D minor 7 chord, you will need to determine how the chord is functioning in the composition. If the chord is functioning as a ii chord (in major), then your choice would be to use mode ii of the major scale (Dorian). If the chord functions as a iii chord, your choice would be Phrygian (mode iii of major). Any minor 7 chord that functions as a vi chord, would require the Aeolian mode (mode vi of major). To fully understand the multiplicity of possible functions a chord can be performing at any specific moment in a piece, one must study harmony.  There are many excellent harmony textbooks available for you to study.  Gordon Delamont's *Modern Harmonic Technique Vols. 1-2* is an excellent starting point.

Our approach to chord-scale relationships is to take any scale and extract a chord built from the root of it.  This chord is viewed as a static chord (i.e., an isolated chord not moving anywhere).

Take any scale and extract the first, third and fifth notes (we will use C as our starting point in the first example and G for the second, but remember that any notes will do, as long as you follow the formulas):

C Lydian $^b$7:     C     D     E     F$^{\#}$     G     A     B$^b$
                    1     2     3     $^{\#}$4     5     6     $^b$7
                    ⇑           ⇑           ⇑

The above scale will yield a C major triad.  If we include the seventh we obtain a C Dominant 7 chord:

C Lydian $^b$7:     C     D     E     F$^{\#}$     G     A     B$^b$
                    1     2     3     $^{\#}$4     5     6     $^b$7
                    ⇑           ⇑           ⇑           ⇑

We can continue the above approach to extract:

C Dom 9             (1 3 5 $^b$7 9)
C Dom 9 $^{\#}$11       (1 3 5 $^b$7 9 $^{\#}$11)
C Dom 13 $^{\#}$11      (1 3 5 $^b$7 9 $^{\#}$11 13)

As a second example consider the following scale:

G Mixolydian $^b$9
          G     A$^b$     B     C     D     E     F
          1     $^b$2     3     4     5     6     $^b$7

A triad built on the root of this scale would be a G major chord.  If a seventh is added, a G Dom 7 chord would be produced. With the addition of upper extensions (9th, 11th and 13th) you can extract:

G Dom 7 $^b$9          (1 3 5 $^b$7 $^b$9)
G Dom 13 $^b$9         (1 3 5 $^b$7 $^b$9 13)

The third and the eleventh create a strong dissonance so in general your best choice is to omit the third if the 4th/11th is present. This would give you:

$$G \text{ sus } 4 \qquad (1 \; 4 \; 5)$$
$$G \text{ Dom } 7 \text{ sus } 4 \qquad (1 \; 4 \; 5 \; {}^b7)$$
$$G \text{ Dom } 7 \; {}^b9 \text{ sus } 4 \quad (1 \; 4 \; 5 \; {}^b7 \; {}^b9)$$
$$G \text{ Dom } 13 \; {}^b9 \text{ sus } 4 \quad (1 \; 4 \; 5 \; {}^b7 \; {}^b9 \; 13)$$

The preceding technique is usually not applied to tetratonic (four note) and pentatonic (five note) scales due to their comparatively disjunct (gapped) intervallic structure. The chords generated from these scales will usually be non-conventional chords (i.e., non-tertian structures). Tetratonic and pentatonic scales are usually harmonized by chords derived from the heptatonic scales. If you do attempt to harmonize these scales and some of the more unusual hexatonic (6 note), heptatonic (7 note), and octatonic (8 note) scales, you will discover some very interesting chords. A quick and easy way to use the less common pentatonic and hexatonic scales, is to compare them with heptatonic scales you already know. For example, the Hirajoshi scale can be thought of as being the Aeolian scale without its fourth and seventh degrees. You can use the Hirajoshi scale where you would normally use the Aeolian scale. The Prometheus scale is the Lydian scale with no fifth scale degree. Therefore, the Prometheus scale could be used in most contexts where a Lydian scale would be appropriate.

You can also build chords on each note of a scale. For example if you were to write out a C major scale and build chords off of each degree, your result would be a harmonized major scale:

**Diatonic Triads**

You can add sevenths to each chord:

**Diatonic Tetrads**

In addition, ninths, elevenths, and thirteenths can be added to each chord.

In the West, the chords derived from the major scale are very important. These chords are used in essentially all styles of popular music. The chords derived from the Natural Minor, Harmonic Minor and Jazz Minor Scales although their use is not as widespread as those their counterparts from the Major Scale, are quite important and warrant investigation. The harmonic materials drawn from these scales are very important in jazz harmony and will provide you with a more sophisticated harmonic vocabulary. This is essential for all improvising musicians and composers.

## Natural Minor Triads

## Natural Minor Tetrads

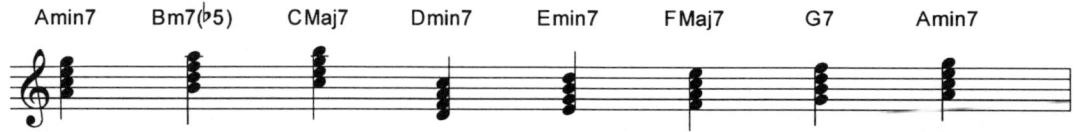

## Harmonic Minor Triads

## Harmonic Minor Tetrads

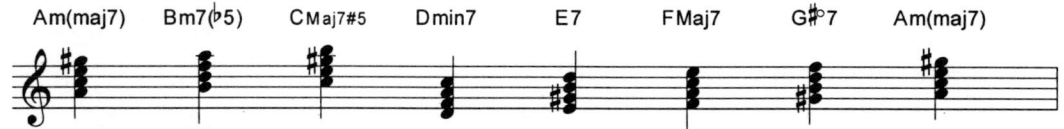

## Jazz Minor Triads

## Jazz Minor Tetrads

Obviously, you can spend many years exploring the almost infinite number of both chordal and modal possibilities for the rather prodigious number of scales in existence. Your best approach is to learn all of the triads and seventh chords in each major, minor, harmonic minor and jazz minor scale. You can then apply your knowledge to the Diatonic and Musica Ficta Modes and beyond.

# Chapter 4 Tetratonic Scales

FOUR NOTE SCALES ARE not very common, but can be heard in some folk music styles.

When they are used, tetratonic scales can usually be thought of as being: a pentatonic scale missing one note, a hexatonic scale missing two notes, or a heptatonic scale missing three notes. To simplify memorization of these scales, look for a scale you are already familiar with that contains the notes of the tetratonic scale. Then simply memorize the tetratonic scale as that scale with the appropriate missing notes.

For example:

| C | F | G | A |
|---|---|---|---|
| 1 | 4 | 5 | 6 |

The above scale can be thought of as being a major scale with its second, third and seventh notes omitted.

Since these scales are relatively uncommon, there are no names to memorize. To build your own tetratonic scales, take any scales you already know and drop out the appropriate amount of notes. This can simply become a game of numbers. If you were to take a heptatonic (seven note) scale and drop out three notes, you will have:

| | |
|---|---|
| 1 2 3 4 | 1 3 4 5 |
| 1 2 3 5 | 1 3 4 6 |
| 1 2 3 6 | 1 3 4 7 |
| 1 2 3 7 | 1 3 5 6 |
| 1 2 4 5 | 1 3 5 7 |
| 1 2 4 6 | 1 3 6 7 |
| 1 2 4 7 | 1 4 5 6 |
| 1 2 5 6 | 1 4 5 7 |
| 1 2 5 7 | 1 4 6 7 |
| 1 2 6 7 | 1 5 6 7 |

Try the above tetratonic versions with every heptatonic scale you can. You can also take any major scale and work it through the above numerical combinations. You should then begin to alter the notes by way of sharps or flats to extract each combination of notes.  The following example uses a C major scale.

For example: 1 4 5 6  (C F G A) can become:

$$C\ F^{\#}\ G\ A$$
$$C\ F^{\#}\ G^{\#}\ A$$
$$C\ F^{\#}\ G^{\#}\ A^{\#}$$
$$C\ F\ G^{\#}\ A$$
$$C\ F\ G^{\#}\ A^{\#}$$
$$C\ F\ G^{b}\ A$$
$$C\ F\ G^{b}\ A^{b}$$
$$C\ F\ G^{b}\ A^{\#}$$
$$C\ F\ G\ A^{\#}$$

As you can see, there are numerous possibilities, so remember that this will be a lifelong process of experimentation.

Many of the combinations of four notes are actually complete or incomplete arpeggios—this is why most scale books do not consider tetratonic scales.  You may find it useful to view some of these scales as such.  The scales that are really just arpeggios can not truly be considered tetratonic scales.  You will however find some fascinating note combinations.  So, it is well worth a detailed examination of some of the many possibilities for tetratonic scales.

Take the scales you like and write them down in a notebook for future reference, then take these scales and incorporate them into your daily practice schedule.

# Chapter 5 — Pentatonic Scales

PENTATONIC SCALES ARE FIVE note scales. There is a plethora of pentatonic scales being used by most cultures of the world. Their use is especially prevalent among East Asian cultures. The most common pentatonic scales used in the West are actually Chinese scales. The Chinese have made extensive use of what is commonly known as the major pentatonic scale and its related modes. The two most common pentatonic scales in the West are the major and minor pentatonic scales. You can hear these scales used extensively in Rock, Country, Blues, Jazz, Folk, Reggae and New Age.

The Chinese Pentatonic scales numbered 1-5 are all modes of the major pentatonic scale.

The Major Pentatonic scale is quite often derived by omitting the IV and vii degrees of the major scale. For example, to build a C major pentatonic scale you would drop the F and B from the C major scale.

**C major:**

| C | D | E | F | G | A | B | C |
|---|---|---|---|---|---|---|---|
|   |   |   | ⇑ |   |   | ⇑ |   |
|   |   |   | IV |   |   | vii |   |

**C major pentatonic:**

*All are made of 3 Ts + 1 T½*

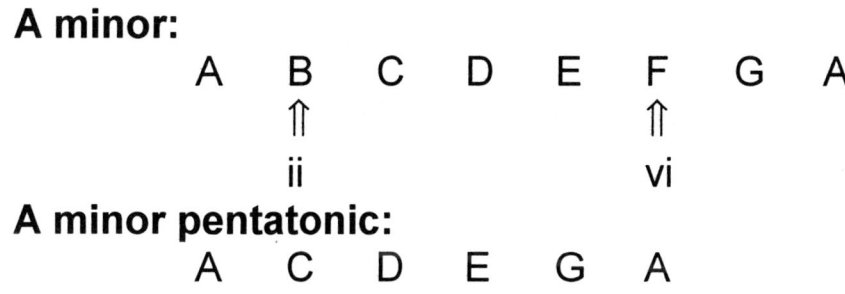

C D E G A C
T T T½ T

The same procedure is often followed for the derivation of the minor pentatonic scale except this time the ii and vi degrees will have to be dropped from the minor scale:

**A minor:**

| A | B | C | D | E | F | G | A |
|---|---|---|---|---|---|---|---|
|   | ⇑ |   |   |   | ⇑ |   |   |
|   | ii |   |   |   | vi |   |   |

**A minor pentatonic:**

A C D E G A

The two notes that are omitted from the major and minor pentatonic scales form the interval of an augmented 4th or a diminished fifth (this interval is also called the *tritone*). With the removal of the tritone any awkwardness in the major or minor scale has been removed thus making pentatonic melodies easy to remember and sing.

If we take a modal approach to these scales our result is as follows:

# Anhemitonic Pentatonic Scales

(Pentatonic scales without semitones)

### Major Pentatonic Mode I

| C | D | E | G | A |
|---|---|---|---|---|
| 1 | 2 | 3 | 5 | 6 |

### Major Pentatonic Mode ii (Sus Pent)

| D | E | G | A | C |
|---|---|---|---|---|
| 1 | 2 | 4 | 5 | $^b7$ |

### Major Pentatonic Mode iii

| E | G | A | C | D |
|---|---|---|---|---|
| 1 | $^b3$ | 4 | $^b6$ | $^b7$ |

### Major Pentatonic Mode IV

| G | A | C | D | E |
|---|---|---|---|---|
| 1 | 2 | 4 | 5 | 6 |

### Major Pentatonic Mode V (Minor Pent)

| A | C | D | E | G |
|---|---|---|---|---|
| 1 | $^b3$ | 4 | 5 | $^b7$ |

Now we will rewrite the above modes so that each commences on a C. This approach will allow you to hear the differences in each scale with ease.

## Mode 1 Major Pentatonic (Chinese Pent Scale No. 1, Mongolian)

C   D   E   G   A
1   2   3   5   6

## Sus 4 Pentatonic (Mode ii Maj Pent, Chinese Pent No. 2, Egyptian)

C   D   F   G   B$^b$
1   2   4   5   $^b$7

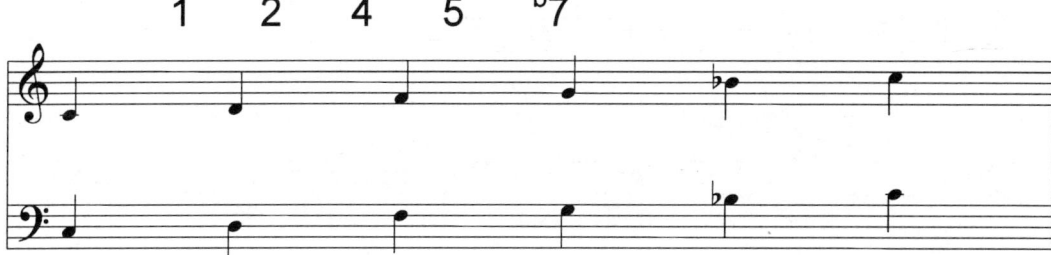

## Mode iii Major Pentatonic (Chinese Pentatonic scale No. 3)

C   E$^b$   F   A$^b$   B$^b$
1   $^b$3   4   $^b$6   $^b$7

### Mode IV Major Pentatonic (Chinese Pentatonic scale No. 4)

| C | D | F | G | A |
|---|---|---|---|---|
| 1 | 2 | 4 | 5 | 6 |

### Minor Pentatonic (Mode V Maj Pent, Chinese Pentatonic scale No. 5)

| C | E$^b$ | F | G | B$^b$ |
|---|---|---|---|---|
| 1 | $^b$3 | 4 | 5 | $^b$7 |

# Hemitonic Pentatonic Scales
(Pentatonic scales with semitones)

### Chinese Pentatonic scale No. 6 (Mode ii Miyako-bushi)

| C | E | F$^\#$ | G | B |
|---|---|---|---|---|
| 1 | 3 | $^\#$4 | 5 | 7 |

## Japanese Pentatonic scale No. 1 (Kumoi-Joshi, Miyako-bushi)

## Hirajoshi (Japanese Pentatonic scale No. 2, Mode iii Miyako-bushi)

## Japanese Pentatonic scale No. 3 (Mode IV Kumoi)

## Iwato (Japanese Pentatonic scale No. 4, Mode IV Miyako-bushi)

| C | D$^b$ | F | G$^b$ | B$^b$ |
|---|---|---|---|---|
| 1 | $^b$2 | 4 | $^b$5 | $^b$7 |

## In (Japanese Pentatonic scale No. 5)

| C | D$^b$ | (E$^b$) | F | G | A$^b$ | (B$^b$) |
|---|---|---|---|---|---|---|
| 1 | $^b$2 | ($^b$3) | 4 | 5 | $^b$6 | ($^b$7) |

The notes shown above in parentheses are auxiliary tones. On the staff below, these auxiliary tones are indicated by noteheads that are represented by X's. Auxiliary tones can best be thought of as being ornamental tones that can be added to the scale for greater melodic variety.

## Yo (Japanese Pentatonic scale No. 6)

| C | D | (E$^b$) | F | G | A | (B$^b$) |
|---|---|---|---|---|---|---|
| 1 | 2 | ($^b$3) | 4 | 5 | 6 | ($^b$7) |

As with the In scale, the notes in parentheses and indicated with X's, are auxiliary tones. They can best be thought of as being ornamental tones that can be added to the scale as desired for greater melodic variety.

## Pélog (Indonesian Pentatonic scale No. 1)

| C | D♭ | E♭ | G | A♭ |
|---|----|----|---|----|
| 1 | ♭2 | ♭3 | 5 | ♭6 |

## Indonesian Pentatonic scale No. 2

| C | D♭ | F♯ | G | A♭ |
|---|----|----|---|----|
| 1 | ♭2 | ♯4 | 5 | ♭6 |

## Indonesian Pentatonic scale No. 3

| C | E | F | G | B |
|---|---|---|---|---|
| 1 | 3 | 4 | 5 | 7 |

## Kumoi scale (Hawaiian)

| C | D | Eb | G | A |
|---|---|----|---|---|
| 1 | 2 | b3 | 5 | 6 |

You can also develop your own pentatonic scales. The only real requirement for a pentatonic scale is that you have a total of five different notes in the scale. You can see that this means there are a multiplicity of possible pentatonic scales. You can create your own pentatonic scales (even although the scales may already exist but may not be widely known) by simply expanding the technique for deriving tetratonic scales that was examined in the preceding chapter.

| | | |
|---|---|---|
| 1 2 3 4 5 | 1 2 3 6 7 | 1 3 4 5 6 |
| 1 2 3 4 6 | 1 2 4 5 6 | 1 3 4 5 7 |
| 1 2 3 4 7 | 1 2 4 5 7 | 1 3 4 6 7 |
| 1 2 3 5 6 | 1 2 4 6 7 | 1 3 5 6 7 |
| 1 2 3 5 7 | 1 2 5 6 7 | 1 4 5 6 7 |

Once you add flats and sharps into the above formulas the scale possibilities will increase exponentially.

You can also take existing pentatonic scales and alter them to suit the chords you wish to improvise over. For example if you wanted a pentatonic scale to use over a Dom 7 b9 b13 chord you can simply formulate the scale you need. Here is one possibility:

$$1 \enspace {}^{b}2 \enspace 3 \enspace {}^{b}6 \enspace {}^{b}7$$

Pentatonic scales such as this are often called *altered* or *hybrid* pentatonic scales.

# Chapter 6 — Hexatonic Scales

A HEXATONIC SCALE IS any scale that has six notes in total. This means that you can take any heptatonic scale (7 note scale) and omit one note or, you could add one note to a pentatonic scale. A point worth noting here is the fact that the tetratonic, pentatonic, and hexatonic scales have been compared to other scales simply for your learning ease. It is important to realize that these scales have their own unique sounds.

## Augmented scale Mode I (Sixtone Symmetrical)

| C | D# | E | G | Ab | B |
|---|----|----|----|----|----|
| 1 | #2 | 3 | 5 | b6 | 7 |
| (1½ | S | 1½ | S | 1½ | S) |

## Augmented scale Mode ii (Sixtone Symmetrical)

| C | Db | E | F | G# | A |
|---|----|----|----|----|----|
| 1 | b2 | 3 | 4 | #5 | 6 |
| (S | 1½ | S | 1½ | S | 1½) |

The Augmented scale, like the Whole-tone scale and the Diminished Whole-half, and the Diminished Half-whole scales, is a symmetrical scale. The augmented scale is constructed by alternating semitones and minor thirds.

## Prometheus

| C | D | E | F# | A | Bb |
|---|---|---|---|---|---|
| 1 | 2 | 3 | #4 | 6 | b7 |

## Prometheus Neapolitan

| C | Db | E | F# | A | Bb |
|---|---|---|---|---|---|
| 1 | b2 | 3 | #4 | 6 | b7 |

## Whole-tone

| C | D | E | F# | G# | Bb |
|---|---|---|---|---|---|
| 1 | 2 | 3 | #4 | #5 | b7 |
| (T | T | T | T | T | T) |

Remember that since the Whole-tone scale is a symmetrical scale, any note can be considered the root note. There are actually only two different Whole-tone scales. (This is because there are twelve notes in total in equal tempered tuning and six of these are found in each Whole-tone scale.)

## Blues

$$C \quad E^b \quad F \quad F^{\#} \quad G \quad B^b$$
$$1 \quad {}^b3 \quad 4 \quad {}^{\#}4 \quad 5 \quad {}^b7$$

This scale can be thought of as being a minor pentatonic scale with an added aug 4/dim 5 ($^{\#}4/^b5$).

## Sus 4

$$C \quad D \quad F \quad G \quad A \quad B^b$$
$$1 \quad 2 \quad 4 \quad 5 \quad 6 \quad {}^b7$$

This scale is mode ii of major pentatonic, with an added major sixth.

# Chapter 7 Hepatonic Scales

SEVEN NOTE SCALES are among the most common scales used throughout the world. Heptatonic scales are the norm for the West. Here is a quick review of the diatonic modes and musica ficta modes.

You should notice that the diatonic modes are written so that they all have the same key signature. In other words, these modes are related via their key signature and hence are referred to as the **relative modes**. This is a good way to look at the modes at first but, due to the fact that most of us have our ears firmly etched in the tonal system of the West, it can be hard to appreciate the subtleties of the modal systems. To really understand the inner workings of each mode, you must examine the modes in **parallel**. Simply apply the formulas that follow so that each mode begins on the note C. For example, to find a C Dorian scale you would need:

$$1 \quad 2 \quad {}^b3 \quad 4 \quad 5 \quad 6 \quad {}^b7$$
$$C \quad D \quad E^b \quad F \quad G \quad A \quad B^b$$

If you now compare the sound of the C Ionian mode to that of C Dorian you will hear quite a difference. To find a C Lydian scale you would need:

$$1 \quad 2 \quad 3 \quad 4^{\#} \quad 5 \quad 6 \quad 7$$
$$C \quad D \quad E \quad F^{\#} \quad G \quad A \quad B$$

A great way to begin to really hear these scales is to practice each scale with a drone. If you play a chordal instrument this is an easy task—simply take the root note and let it resonate for a period of time. If you play piano, play the root notes with your left hand and practice the scale with your right. For those of you that play a monophonic instrument, you can record yourself sustaining a C. You can then go back to practice and improvise with the scale on top of the drone. Be sure to record your drone for at least five minutes.

# Diatonic Modes

## Relative Modes

### Mode I Ionian

| C | D | E | F | G | A | B |
|---|---|---|---|---|---|---|
| 1 | 2 | 3 | 4 | 5 | 6 | 7 |

### Mode ii Dorian

| D | E | F | G | A | B | C |
|---|---|---|---|---|---|---|
| 1 | 2 | $\flat$3 | 4 | 5 | 6 | $\flat$7 |

### Mode iii Phrygian

| E | F | G | A | B | C | D |
|---|---|---|---|---|---|---|
| 1 | $\flat$2 | $\flat$3 | 4 | 5 | $\flat$6 | $\flat$7 |

### Mode IV Lydian

| F | G | A | B | C | D | E |
|---|---|---|---|---|---|---|
| 1 | 2 | 3 | $\sharp$4 | 5 | 6 | 7 |

### Mode V Mixolydian

| G | A | B | C | D | E | F |
|---|---|---|---|---|---|---|
| 1 | 2 | 3 | 4 | 5 | 6 | $\flat$7 |

### Mode vi Aeolian

| A | B | C | D | E | F | G |
|---|---|---|---|---|---|---|
| 1 | 2 | $\flat$3 | 4 | 5 | $\flat$6 | $\flat$7 |

### Mode vii Locrian

| B | C | D | E | F | G | A |
|---|---|---|---|---|---|---|
| 1 | $\flat$2 | $\flat$3 | 4 | $\flat$5 | $\flat$6 | $\flat$7 |

## Parallel Modes
## Mode I Ionian

## Mode ii Dorian

## Mode iii Phrygian

## Mode IV Lydian

| C | D | E | F# | G | A | B |
|---|---|---|---|---|---|---|
| 1 | 2 | 3 | #4 | 5 | 6 | 7 |

## Mode V Mixolydian

| C | D | E | F | G | A | Bb |
|---|---|---|---|---|---|---|
| 1 | 2 | 3 | 4 | 5 | 6 | b7 |

## Mode vi Aeolian

| C | D | Eb | F | G | Ab | Bb |
|---|---|---|---|---|---|---|
| 1 | 2 | b3 | 4 | 5 | b6 | b7 |

## Mode vii Locrian

| C | D$^b$ | E$^b$ | F | G$^b$ | A$^b$ | B$^b$ |
|---|---|---|---|---|---|---|
| 1 | $^b$2 | $^b$3 | 4 | $^b$5 | $^b$6 | $^b$7 |

# Harmonic Minor Modes

## Relative Modes

**Mode I    Harmonic Minor:**

| A | B | C | D | E | F | G$^\#$ |
|---|---|---|---|---|---|---|
| 1 | 2 | $^b$3 | 4 | 5 | $^b$6 | 7 |

**Mode ii    Locrian Natural 6:**

| B | C | D | E | F | G$^\#$ | A |
|---|---|---|---|---|---|---|
| 1 | $^b$2 | $^b$3 | 4 | $^b$5 | 6 | $^b$7 |

**Mode iii    Ionian Augmented:**

| C | D | E | F | G$^\#$ | A | B |
|---|---|---|---|---|---|---|
| 1 | 2 | 3 | 4 | $^\#$5 | 6 | 7 |

**Mode IV    Dorian $^\#$4:**

| D | E | F | G$^\#$ | A | B | C |
|---|---|---|---|---|---|---|
| 1 | 2 | $^b$3 | $^\#$4 | 5 | 6 | $^b$7 |

**Mode V    Mixolydian $^b$9 $^b$13:**

| E | F | G$^\#$ | A | B | C | D |
|---|---|---|---|---|---|---|
| 1 | $^b$2 | 3 | 4 | 5 | $^b$6 | $^b$7 |

**Mode vi   Lydian #9:**

| F | G# | A | B | C | D | E |
|---|----|---|---|---|---|---|
| 1 | #2 | 3 | #4 | 5 | 6 | 7 |

**Mode vii   Altered Dominant bb7:**

| G# | A | B | C | D | E | F |
|----|---|---|---|---|---|---|
| 1 | b2 | b3 | b4 | b5 | b6 | bb7 |

## Parallel Modes
**Mode I   Harmonic Minor:**

| C | D | Eb | F | G | Ab | B |
|---|---|----|---|---|----|---|
| 1 | 2 | b3 | 4 | 5 | b6 | 7 |

**Mode ii   Locrian Natural 6:**

| C | Db | Eb | F | Gb | A | Bb |
|---|----|----|---|----|---|----|
| 1 | b2 | b3 | 4 | b5 | 6 | b7 |

## Mode iii   Ionian Augmented:

| C | D | E | F | G# | A | B |
|---|---|---|---|----|---|---|
| 1 | 2 | 3 | 4 | #5 | 6 | 7 |

## Mode IV   Dorian #4:

| C | D | Eb | F# | G | A | Bb |
|---|---|----|----|---|---|----|
| 1 | 2 | b3 | #4 | 5 | 6 | b7 |

## Mode V   Mixolydian b9 b13:

| C | Db | E | F | G | Ab | Bb |
|---|----|---|---|---|----|----|
| 1 | b2 | 3 | 4 | 5 | b6 | b7 |

**Mode vi   Lydian #9:**

| C | D# | E | F# | G | A | B |
|---|----|---|----|---|---|---|
| 1 | #2 | 3 | #4 | 5 | 6 | 7 |

**Mode vii   Altered Dominant bb7:**

| C | Db | Eb | Fb | Gb | Ab | Bbb |
|---|----|----|----|----|----|-----|
| 1 | b2 | b3 | b4 | b5 | b6 | bb7 |

# Jazz Minor Modes

**Relative Modes**

**Mode I   Jazz Minor:**

| A | B | C | D | E | F# | G# |
|---|---|---|---|---|----|----|
| 1 | 2 | b3 | 4 | 5 | 6 | 7 |

**Mode ii   Dorian b2:**

| B | C | D | E | F# | G# | A |
|---|---|---|---|----|----|---|
| 1 | b2 | b3 | 4 | 5 | 6 | b7 |

**Mode iii   Lydian Augmented:**

| C | D | E | F$^\sharp$ | G$^\sharp$ | A | B |
|---|---|---|---|---|---|---|
| 1 | 2 | 3 | $^\sharp$4 | $^\sharp$5 | 6 | 7 |

**Mode IV   Lydian $^\flat$7:**

| D | E | F$^\sharp$ | G$^\sharp$ | A | B | C |
|---|---|---|---|---|---|---|
| 1 | 2 | 3 | $^\sharp$4 | 5 | 6 | $^\flat$7 |

**Mode V   Mixolydian $^\flat$13:**

| E | F$^\sharp$ | G$^\sharp$ | A | B | C | D |
|---|---|---|---|---|---|---|
| 1 | 2 | 3 | 4 | 5 | $^\flat$6 | $^\flat$7 |

**Mode vi   Locrian Natural 9:**

| F$^\sharp$ | G$^\sharp$ | A | B | C | D | E |
|---|---|---|---|---|---|---|
| 1 | 2 | $^\flat$3 | 4 | $^\flat$5 | $^\flat$6 | $^\flat$7 |

**Mode vii   Altered Dominant:** You should note that this mode is often spelled with enharmonicism. (*Enharmonicism* is the re-spelling of a note a second way.) In equal tempered tuning there is no difference in sound between an F$^\sharp$ and a G$^\flat$. The Altered Dominant mode would be spelled as: 1 $^\flat$2 $^\flat$3 $^\flat$4 $^\flat$5 $^\flat$6 $^\flat$7 if you were to derive it from the Jazz Minor scale. This scale is also referred to as the *Super Locrian* scale.

| G$^\sharp$ | A | B | C | D | E | F$^\sharp$ |
|---|---|---|---|---|---|---|
| 1 | $^\flat$2 | $^\flat$3 | $^\flat$4 | $^\flat$5 | $^\flat$6 | $^\flat$7 |

If this scale is derived in relation to its perceived dominant function (it is usually referred to as the *Altered Dominant* scale), the following formula will result:

| G$^\sharp$ | A | A$^x$ | B$^\sharp$ | C$^x$ | D$^x$ | F$^\sharp$ |
|---|---|---|---|---|---|---|
| 1 | $^\flat$2 | $^\sharp$2 | 3 | $^\sharp$4 | $^\sharp$5 | $^\flat$7 |

## Parallel Modes
### Mode I    Jazz Minor:

| C | D | E♭ | F | G | A | B |
|---|---|-----|---|---|---|---|
| 1 | 2 | ♭3 | 4 | 5 | 6 | 7 |

### Mode ii    Dorian ♭2:

| C | D♭ | E♭ | F | G | A | B♭ |
|---|-----|-----|---|---|---|-----|
| 1 | ♭2 | ♭3 | 4 | 5 | 6 | ♭7 |

### Mode iii   Lydian Augmented:

| C | D | E | F♯ | G♯ | A | B |
|---|---|---|-----|-----|---|---|
| 1 | 2 | 3 | ♯4 | ♯5 | 6 | 7 |

## Mode IV   Lydian $^b$7:

| C | D | E | F# | G | A | B$^b$ |
|---|---|---|----|---|---|-------|
| 1 | 2 | 3 | #4 | 5 | 6 | $^b$7 |

## Mode V   Mixolydian $^b$13:

| C | D | E | F | G | A$^b$ | B$^b$ |
|---|---|---|---|---|-------|-------|
| 1 | 2 | 3 | 4 | 5 | $^b$6 | $^b$7 |

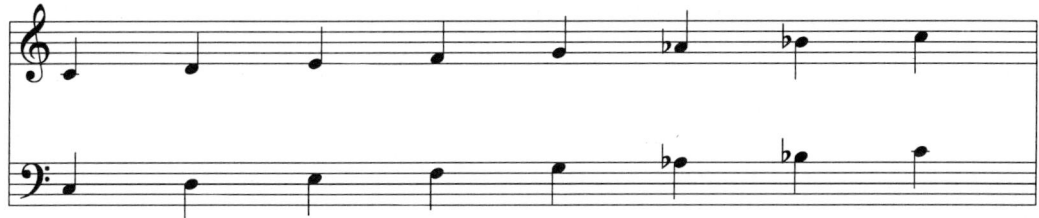

## Mode vi   Locrian Natural 9:

| C | D | E$^b$ | F | G$^b$ | A$^b$ | B$^b$ |
|---|---|-------|---|-------|-------|-------|
| 1 | 2 | $^b$3 | 4 | $^b$5 | $^b$6 | $^b$7 |

## Mode vii  Altered Dominant:

| C | D♭ | D♯ | E | F♯ | G♯ | B♭ |
|---|----|----|----|----|----|----|
| 1 | ♭2 | ♯2 | 3 | ♯4 | ♯5 | ♭7 |

The following scales represent some of the musica ficta modes. These scales have been re-written below to indicate some of their many possible synonyms.

## Tarz-nwin (Locrian nat 6, Mode ii Harmonic Minor)

| C | D♭ | E♭ | F | G♭ | A | B♭ |
|---|----|----|----|----|----|----|
| 1 | ♭2 | ♭3 | 4 | ♭5 | 6 | ♭7 |

## Hejaz (Mixolydian ♭9 ♭13, Mode V Harmonic Minor, Phrygian Major, Phrygian Dominant, Spanish, Gypsy)

| C | D♭ | E | F | G | A♭ | B♭ |
|---|----|----|----|----|----|----|
| 1 | ♭2 | 3 | 4 | 5 | ♭6 | ♭7 |

## Nikris (Dorian #4, Mode IV Harmonic Minor, Rumanian Minor)

$$
\begin{array}{ccccccc}
C & D & E^b & F^\# & G & A & B^b \\
1 & 2 & {}^b3 & {}^\#4 & 5 & 6 & {}^b7
\end{array}
$$

## Lydian ♭7 (Mode IV Jazz Minor, Overtone scale, Mixolydian #4, Lydian Dominant)

$$
\begin{array}{ccccccc}
C & D & E & F^\# & G & A & B^b \\
1 & 2 & 3 & {}^\#4 & 5 & 6 & {}^b7
\end{array}
$$

## Musta-ar (Lydian #9, Mode vi Harmonic Minor)

$$
\begin{array}{ccccccc}
C & D^\# & E & F^\# & G & A & B \\
1 & {}^\#2 & 3 & {}^\#4 & 5 & 6 & 7
\end{array}
$$

## Javanese (Mode ii Jazz Minor, Dorian ♭2)

## Hindustan (Mixolydian ♭6, Mixolydian ♭13,  Mode V Jazz Minor, Hindu)

The following heptatonic scales provide some truly unique sounds.  If you are still looking for more scales after you complete this section you should modalize these scales and/or apply the scale formation techniques we examined in the preceding chapters.

## Hejaz-Kar (Byzantine, Double Harmonic, Gypsy)

**Purvi**

**Todi**

**Saba**

## Hungarian Major (Hungarian)

| C | D# | E | F# | G | A | Bb |
|---|----|---|----|---|---|----|
| 1 | #2 | 3 | #4 | 5 | 6 | b7 |

## Hungarian Gypsy No. 1 (Hungarian Minor, Mode IV Hejaz-Kar)

| C | D | Eb | F# | G | Ab | B |
|---|---|----|----|---|----|---|
| 1 | 2 | b3 | #4 | 5 | b6 | 7 |

## Hungarian Gypsy No. 2

| C | D | Eb | F# | G | Ab | Bb |
|---|---|----|----|---|----|----|
| 1 | 2 | b3 | #4 | 5 | b6 | b7 |

The two so-called Hungarian Gypsy scales seen above have been numbered one and two respectively to indicate that they are different scales. The problem encountered here is that when someone refers to the Hungarian Gypsy scale, there is no way of knowing which of the above they are referring to. Both versions appear in textbooks as the Hungarian Gypsy scale.

## Harmonic Major  (Suzinak)

## Spanish Dominant (Mode iii Harmonic Major)

## Smyrneiko (Mode IV Harmonic Major)

## Mixolydian ♭9 (Mode V Harmonic Major)

| C | D♭ | E | F | G | A | B♭ |
|---|---|---|---|---|---|---|
| 1 | ♭2 | 3 | 4 | 5 | 6 | ♭7 |

## Enigmatic

| C | D♭ | E | F♯ | G♯ | A♯ | B |
|---|---|---|---|---|---|---|
| 1 | ♭2 | 3 | ♯4 | ♯5 | ♯6 | 7 |

## Major Locrian (Arabian)

| C | D | E | F | G♭ | A♭ | B♭ |
|---|---|---|---|---|---|---|
| 1 | 2 | 3 | 4 | ♭5 | ♭6 | ♭7 |

## Lydian Minor   (Mode vii Major Locrian)

| C | D | E | F# | G | Ab | Bb |
|---|---|---|----|---|----|----|
| 1 | 2 | 3 | #4 | 5 | b6 | b7 |

## Leading Whole-tone (Mode V Major Locrian)

| C | D | E | F# | G# | A# | B |
|---|---|---|----|----|----|---|
| 1 | 2 | 3 | #4 | #5 | #6 | 7 |

## Persian (Mode V Todi)

| C | Db | E | F | Gb | Ab | B |
|---|----|---|---|----|----|---|
| 1 | b2 | 3 | 4 | b5 | b6 | 7 |

## Oriental No. 1(Mode ii Hungarian Gypsy No. 2)

| C | D♭ | E | F | G♭ | A♭ | B♭ |
|---|---|---|---|---|---|---|
| 1 | ♭2 | 3 | 4 | ♭5 | ♭6 | ♭7 |

## Oriental No. 2 (Mode V Hejaz-Kar)

| C | D♭ | E | F | G♭ | A | B♭ |
|---|---|---|---|---|---|---|
| 1 | ♭2 | 3 | 4 | ♭5 | 6 | ♭7 |

## Neapolitan Major (Mode IV Major Locrian)

| C | D♭ | E♭ | F | G | A | B♭ |
|---|---|---|---|---|---|---|
| 1 | ♭2 | ♭3 | 4 | 5 | 6 | 7 |

## Neapolitan Minor (Harmonic Phrygian, Mode V Hungarian Gypsy No. 2)

| C | D♭ | E♭ | F | G | A♭ | B |
|---|----|----|---|---|----|----|
| 1 | ♭2 | ♭3 | 4 | 5 | ♭6 | 7 |

## Composite Blues

| C | E♭ | E | F | F♯ | G | B♭ |
|---|----|---|---|----|---|----|
| 1 | ♭3 | 3 | 4 | ♯4 | 5 | ♭7 |

# Chapter 8 — Miscellany

## Octatonic Scales

OCTATONIC (EIGHT NOTE) SCALES are not very common. We will examine the three main types—Half-whole Diminished, Whole-half Diminished, Bebop—plus the Japanese Ichikotsucho scale.

  The two Diminished scales are *octave species* or modes of each other. These scales divide the octave into equidistant intervals, and are sometimes called *symmetrical* or *synthetic* scales.

### Whole-half Diminished (Arabian)

The Whole-half Diminished scale is a symmetrical scale that is constructed from the following interval pattern: T   S   T   S   T   S   T   S

| 1 | 2 | $^b$3 | 4 | $^{\#}$4/$^b$5 | $^{\#}$5/$^b$6 | 6 | 7 |
|---|---|---|---|---|---|---|---|
| C | D | E$^b$ | F | F$^{\#}$ | G$^{\#}$ | A | B |

### Half-whole Diminished

The Half-whole Diminished scale is constructed of alternating semitones and whole tones: S   T   S   T   S   T   S   T

## Half-whole Diminished

| 1 | b2 | b3 | 3 | #4/b5 | 5 | 6 | b7 |
|---|----|----|---|-------|---|---|-----|
| C | Db | Eb | E | F# | G | A | Bb |

## Japanese (Ichikotsucho)

| C | D | E | F | F# | G | A | B |
|---|---|---|---|----|---|---|---|
| 1 | 2 | 3 | 4 | #4 | 5 | 6 | 7 |

## The Bebop Scale:

## Major Bebop

| C | D | E | F | G | G# | A | B |
|---|---|---|---|---|----|---|---|
| 1 | 2 | 3 | 4 | 5 | #5 | 6 | 7 |

## Dorian Bebop

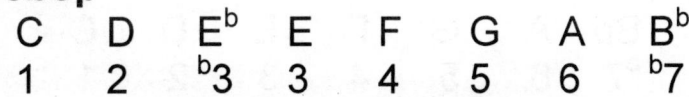

## Mixolydian Bebop No. 1

Some forms of the Bebop scale have different ascending and descending forms.

## Mixolydian Bebop No. 2

Ascending

## Descending

| B | Bb | A | G | F | E | D | C |
|---|----|----|----|----|----|----|----|
| 7 | b7 | 6 | 5 | 4 | 3 | 2 | 1 |

Here are the ascending and descending forms of the Mixolydian Bebop No. 2 combined.

Nine, ten and eleven note scales are not common. You may however choose to build your own nine, ten, or eleven note scales. If this is the case, use the information you have accumulated thus far to generate some of the numerous possibilities.

You will encounter a scale that consists of all twelve notes. This is the *Chromatic scale*.

# The Chromatic Scale

The Chromatic scale is a scale that contains all 12 notes. The scale consists of: S S S S S S S S S S S S. If the twelve notes are utilized so that each note is of equal importance you have the *Dodecaphonic, Duodecuple, or the twelve tone* scale. The above names are sometimes used interchangeably.

C C# D D# E F F# G G# A A# B C

# Index

# ALSO AVAILABLE FROM AGOGIC PUBLISHING

## MUSIC ESSENTIALS: IMPROVISER
ISBN 1-896595-23-5  
$7.99 CDN $6.99 USD  
1 DOUBLE SIDED PAGE  

11 X 17  
2 COLOURS BLUE AND SILVER  
LAMINATED REFERENCE CHART  

MUSIC ESSENTIALS: IMPROVISER provides the intermediate musician with the tools to improvise over chords. Start with a scale and view the chords that can be used or, select a chord and view its scale options. All scales are shown in both treble and bass clefs. The Improviser is the first chart to provide musicians with easy access to this information.

## GUITAR ESSENTIALS: IMPROVISER
ISBN 1-896595-19-7  
$7.99 CDN $6.99 USD  
1 DOUBLE SIDED PAGE  

11 X 17  
2 COLOURS BLACK AND GOLD  
LAMINATED REFERENCE CHART  

GUITAR ESSENTIALS: IMPROVISER provides the intermediate guitarist with the tools to improvise over chords. Start with a scale and view the chords that can be used or, select a chord and view its scale options. All scale forms are shown in transposable neck diagrams. The Improviser is the first chart to provide guitar players with easy access to this information.

## GUITAR ESSENTIALS: CHORD MASTER
ISBN 1-896595-13-8  
$4.99 CDN $3.99 USD  
1 DOUBLE SIDED PAGE  

8½ X 11  
2 COLOURS BLACK AND RED  
LAMINATED REFERENCE CHART  

GUITAR ESSENTIALS: THE CHORD MASTER shows guitarists of all levels how to quickly and easily play 1176 of the most common guitar chords.

## GUITAR ESSENTIALS: SCALE MASTER 1
ISBN 1-896595-11-1  
$4.99 CDN $3.99 USD  
1 DOUBLE SIDED PAGE  

8½ X 11  
2 COLOURS BLACK AND RED  
LAMINATED REFERENCE CHART  

GUITAR ESSENTIALS: THE SCALE MASTER 1 shows you how to play the most common scales. Major, minor, harmonic minor, melodic minor, major pentatonic, minor pentatonic, blues and the composite blues scales are all included in this chart.

## WORLD OF SCALES: A COMPENDIUM OF SCALES FOR THE MODERN GUITAR PLAYER
ISBN 1-896595-07-3  
$25.95 CDN $19.95 USD  
8½ X 11  

165 PAGES  
AUTHOR: DON J. MACLEAN  
EDITOR: ROB BOWMAN PH.D.  

THE WORLD OF SCALES: A COMPENDIUM OF SCALES FOR THE MODERN GUITAR PLAYER shows guitarists of all levels how scales can be used. The World of Scales provides the reader with the most comprehensive examination of scales available. All scales are shown in easy-to-read and transposable fingerings.

## WORLD OF SCALES: A COMPENDIUM OF SCALES FOR ALL INSTRUMENTS 2ND EDITION

ISBN 1-896595-21-9                          96 PAGES
$25.95 CDN $19.95 USD                        AUTHOR: DON J. MACLEAN
8½ X 11

THE WORLD OF SCALES: A COMPENDIUM OF SCALES FOR ALL INSTRUMENTS enables intermediate to advanced musicians to understand: how scales are built; how chords are constructed and interact with scales; and how to apply modalization to any scale. The World of Scales provides the reader with the most thorough examination of scales available. All scales are shown in treble and bass clefs.

## LEARNING THE GUITAR BEGINNERS PACKAGE

ISBN 1-894044-85-1                          60 MIN VHS
$29.95                                       COMPANION AUDIO CD
STUDIES AND PIECES 56 PAGE BOOK             AUTHOR: MICHAEL GILLETTE

LEARNING THE GUITAR BEGINNERS PACKAGE is the ultimate resource for the beginning guitarist. The package includes the video: **Learning the Guitar Expanded Edition**, the book: **Studies and Pieces for the Advancing Guitarist** and the companion audio CD: **Studies and Pieces for the Advancing Guitarist**. This package will take the beginner from tuning the instrument to playing music.

## LEARNING THE GUITAR: CHILDREN'S EDITION

27 MIN. VHS                                 AUTHOR: MICHAEL GILLETTE
$14.95

Designed as a first lesson, this video covers tuning notes, guitar parts, basic fingering technique, and single note playing. The material, while being technically sound, covers a limited range on the guitar. This makes it ideal for smaller hands. Demonstrations of four pieces are made by a young child.

## LEARNING THE UKULELE

27 MIN. VHS                                 AUTHOR: MICHAEL GILLETTE
$14.95

The Ukulele is a wonderfully versatile instrument for music lovers of all ages. On this 27 minute video, Michael Gillette shows the parts of the instrument, tuning, fingering, basic chords, rhythms and single note playing. The pieces are drawn from both popular and Polynesian music. This is a great way to start on this fun instrument.

# ORDER FORM

Canadian residents, prices shown in Canadian funds.

| Title | Price + GST | Shipping | Sub total | Qty. | Total |
|---|---|---|---|---|---|
| World of Scales: A Compendium of Scales for the Modern Guitar Player | $25.95+$1.95 | $5.00 | $32.90 | | |
| World of Scales: A Compendium of Scales for all Instruments | $25.95+$1.95 | $5.00 | $32.90 | | |
| Guitar Essentials: Chord Master | $4.99+$0.38 | $2.00 | $7.37 | | |
| Guitar Essentials: Scale Master 1 | $4.99+$0.38 | $2.00 | $7.37 | | |
| Guitar Essentials: Improviser | $7.99+$0.56 | $2.00 | $7.37 | | |
| Music Essentials: Improviser | $7.99+$0.56 | $2.00 | $7.37 | | |
| | | | Grand total | | |

Discounts available on bulk orders. For information fax 604-540-4419

US residents, prices shown in US funds.

| Title | Price | Shipping | Sub total | Qty. | Total |
|---|---|---|---|---|---|
| World of Scales: A Compendium of Scales for the Modern Guitar Player | $19.95 | $6.00 | $25.95 | | |
| World of Scales: A Compendium of Scales for all Instruments | $12.99 | $5.00 | $17.99 | | |
| Guitar Essentials: Chord Master | $3.99 | $2.00 | $5.99 | | |
| Guitar Essentials: Scale Master 1 | $3.99 | $2.00 | $5.99 | | |
| Guitar Essentials: Improviser | $6.99 | $2.00 | $8.99 | | |
| Music Essentials: Improviser | $6.99 | $2.00 | $8.99 | | |
| | | | Grand total | | |

Discounts available on bulk orders. For information fax 604-540-4419

**Ship To:**

Name _____

Address _____

City/ Prov/State _____

Postal/Zip Code _____

Phone _____

Email _____

Mail this order form today with your money order payable to:

**Agogic Publishing**
406-109 Tenth Street
New Westminster, BC
V3M 3X7
Phone 604-290-2692
Fax 604-540-4419

Please cut along dotted line.